DAVE STRYKER'S
JAZZ GUITAR IMPROVISATION METHOD

D1528934

Cover photo by Jimmy Katz

Audio Contents

Guitar and Bass – Dave Stryker • Drums – Eric Halvorson • Recorded at Strikezone Studio

1	The Minor Sub Approach Ex. 1
2	Ex. 2
3	Ex. 3
4	Ex. 4
5	Ex. 5
6	Ex. 6a
7	Ex. 6b
8	Ex. 6c
9	Ex. 7
10	Ex. 8
11	Ex. 8a
12	Ex. 8b
13	Solo ideas for "Autumn Leaves" (slow)
14	Rhythm track w/o solo for #13
15	Solo ideas for "Autumn Leaves" (med)
16	Rhythm track w/o solo for #15
17	Solo ideas for "Well You Needn't"
18	Rhythm track w/o solo for #17
19	Minor Sub Arp. Blues
20	Rhythm track for #19
21	Min. Sub Arp. blues w/1/2 step app.
22	Rhythm track for #21
23	Blues #1
24	Rhythm track for #23
25	F blues scale
26	Blues #2
27	Rhythm track for #26
28	Blues #3

29	Rhythm track for #28
30	F blues scale
31	F minor arpeggio
32	Solo ideas for "Song for my Father"
33	Rhythm track for #32
34	E♭ Major Pentatonic
35	C minor Pentatonic
36	Solo ideas for "Blue Bossa"
37	Rhythm track for #36
38	Turnarounds #1
39	#2
40	#3
41	#4
42	#5
43	#6
44	#7
45	#8
46	#9
47	#10
48	Solo ideas for "Afternoon in Paris"
49	Rhythm track for #48
50	Melodic Minor Scale
51	Ex. 1
52	Ex. 2
53	Ex. 3
54	Whole Tone Scale
55	Ex. 1
56	Ex. 2

57	Ex. 3
58	Ex. 4
59	Ex. 5
60	Diminished Scale #1
61	#2
62	#3
63	#4
64	#5
65	#6
66	#7
67	#8
68	C Minor Blues
69	Rhythm track for #68
70	Solo ideas for "All the Things You Are"
71	Rhythm track for #70
72	Solo ideas for "Rhythm Changes"
73	Rhythm track for #72
74	Solo ideas for "Cherokee"
75	Rhythm track for #74
76	"Giant Steps"
77	Solo ideas for "Giant Steps"
78	Rhythm track for #77
79	Hanon-type warm-up exercises #1
80	#2
81	#3
82	#4
83	#5

"Dave has done a great job of laying out basic ideas that jazz players use to make their music distinct. Being the master guitarist he is, Dave's concise ways of showing the basics of jazz guitar will help the student create jazz lines that are flowing and original. This is a welcomed addition to the jazz guitar books library."

Jamey Aebersold

Online Audio

www.melbay.com/21114BCDEB

MEL BAY ®

1 2 3 4 5 6 7 8 9 0

Visit us on the Web at www.melbay.com — E-mail us at email@melbay.com

CONTENTS

NOTES FROM DAVE

This book is a method I have been working on for the last few years to help my students develop improvisational ideas when playing jazz. I have included my fingerings above the tab, as it is important for the phrasing. Put your hand in the position that is listed. For example, in the 3rd position, your first finger is on the third fret of the guitar. Then use one finger per fret, following the fingering numbers. I usually use alternate picking, but with occasional slurs and pull-offs to make the phrasing more horn-like and swinging. Please also try and read the notes, as reading music is important to being a well-rounded musician. Good Luck and I hope this book opens the door to helping you to develop some ideas of your own. Also remember: the key to improving, moving to the next level, and eventually developing your own sound, is in listening and transcribing the solos of the master's.

I'd like to thank my friend and fellow guitarist, Herbie Maitlandt, for his help in putting this book together on the computer. Thanks also to Corey Christiansen, Bill Bay, everyone at Mel Bay and Jamey Aebersold. I'd also like to thank my teachers, especially Billy Rogers and Ron Cooley, and the jazz guitar greats who inspired me: Grant Green, Wes Montgomery, Pat Martino, George Benson, Jim Hall, Joe Pass, and on and on…. Also thanks to Jack McDuff and Stanley Turrentine who taught me on the bandstand.

Dave Stryker

To contact Dave or for more information visit www.davestryker.com

OFTEN ASKED QUESTIONS ABOUT MUSIC

Where do I get musical ideas from?
1. Listen to the masters of the guitar.
2. Listen to the masters of <u>all</u> instruments.
3. **PRACTICE!**
   A. Transcribe (make a tape of each solo you learn).
   B. Learn Be-Bop melodies (heads) of the masters (Bird, Monk, etc.).
   C. Learn Standards.
   D. Practice playing Standards with a metronome or a play-a-long recording.
   E. Work on sight-reading a little everyday.
   F. Keep doing No. 1 and 2, all the time (It will rub off!)
   G. Organize jam sessions with other players.
   H. Do any gigs.
   I. Try writing your own songs based on a standard or your own chord progressions.

How do I become more musical when soloing?
1. <u>Listen</u> to the musicians you're playing with and try to react and create a dialogue.
2. <u>Don't overplay</u> – try to use space to create a tension and release effect.
3. Refer to the <u>melody</u> occasionally. Sometimes the melody might be the strongest thing you can say.
4. Try to tell a story. <u>Start simply</u> and <u>build</u> your solo to a peak.
5. Never forget to play with <u>feeling and heart and use the blues.</u>

The Minor Sub Approach

When improvising over a dominant seventh chord I think of the minor scale that relates to it.
For example: play the minor scale starting a fifth above (or a fourth below) the root of the dominant seventh chord. In jazz we almost always use the Dorian minor (minor scale with a raised 6th). A C Dorian scale is the logical choice for a F7 chord. I call this approach (finding the minor scale that works against different chords) the Minor Substitution or Minor sub Approach.
I first heard this approach when I began learning how to play jazz by listening to Grant Green, Wes Montgomery and Pat Martino.

Chord - Scale Chart for the Minor Sub Approach

4

Passing Tones

When playing jazz you sometimes use notes that are not in the scale to connect ideas. These notes are called passing tones. In this book you'll find some chromatic ideas as well as approach notes. In the following examples I use B natural as the approach note to the C dorian ideas in the first examples. The approach note is often times on the "and" of the 4th beat in the last measure before the new phrase. I also show some half-diminished and major seventh chord scale ideas, and some tri-tone ideas. These ideas can be seen in a solo written over the changes to the standard "Autumn Leaves".

The Minor Sub Approach

Dave Stryker

When playing on a Dominant 7th chord (V7) think of the relative II minor. For instance, on F7 think of C minor:

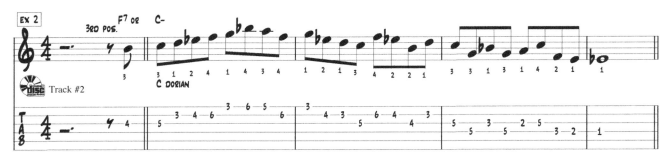

A II - V - I run in the key of Bb:

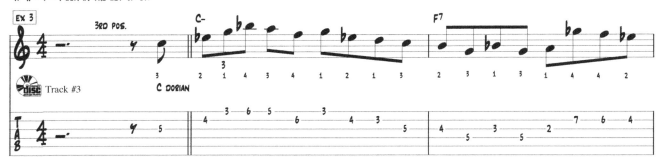

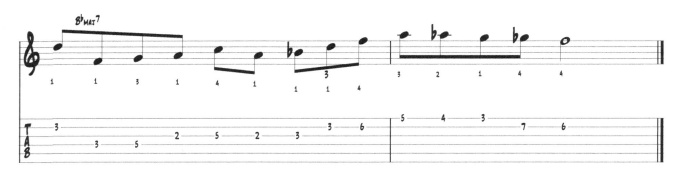

Half-Diminished Chords

Another common chord in jazz is the half-diminished chord (also called a minor 7 flat 5 chord). It is a minor chord with a flatted fifth. It is usually the II chord in a minor II/V/I. And is followed by a dominant 7th altered chord a 4th above. For instance: A-7b5/D7+9/G-7. A-7b5 can also be written as A∅

On a half-diminished chord (minor 7 flat 5) play the minor sound up a minor third from the root: Over A-7b5 play C- ideas (the 1st measure of ex. 1-3) (*Also use C melodic minor over A∅ (see pg.26))

Also On a half-diminished chord (minor 7 flat 5), you can play the (whole-half diminished scale)

Major Seventh Chords

Major 7th Chord ideas: (Bb major scale same as F dom mixolydian)

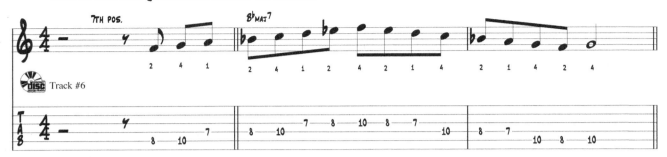

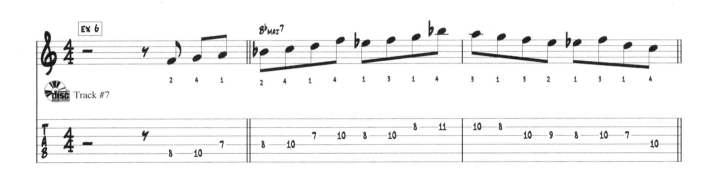

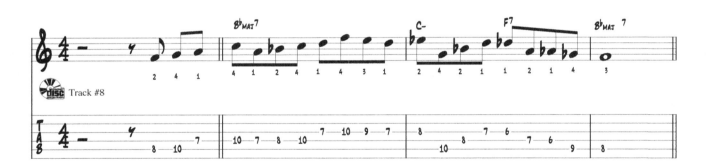

A tri-tone is a raised fourth interval. On a F7 chord the tri-tone substitution would be a B7 chord.
Using our minor-sub approach we can now play over /C-/ F7 /Bb△/
tri-tone sub/C-/F#- B7/Bb△/

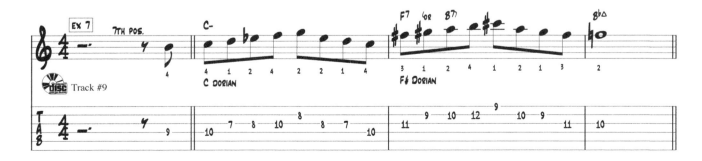

8

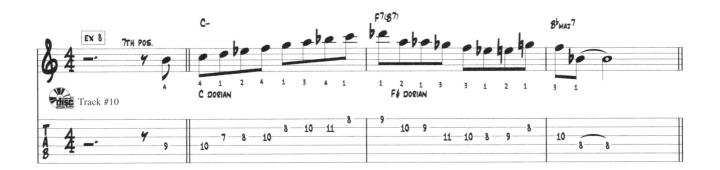

Approach a chord from a half-step above using the same chord. Example: approach C- from C#- or C maj from C# maj
Or: Do the same thing but use a dominant 7 chord a half-step above: approach C- or C maj from C#7

Solo Ideas for Autumn Leaves

Dave Stryker

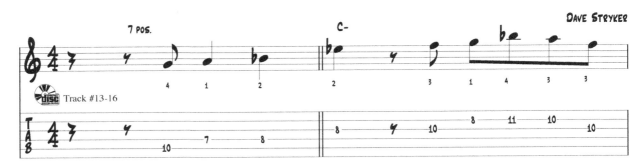

Track #13-16

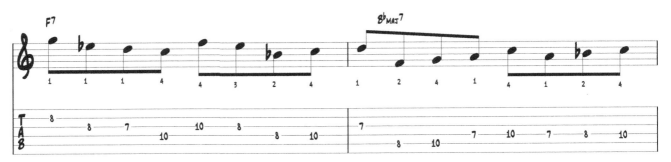

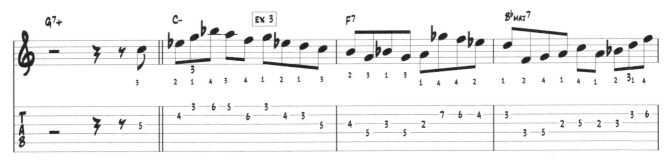

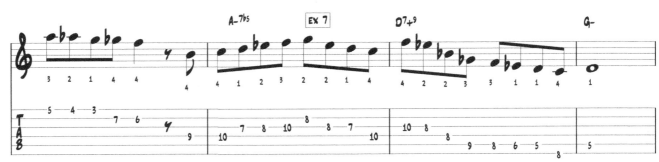

Tip from Dave: Play this solo on "Autumn Leaves" slowly at first. Use a metronome set at around 80 for quarter notes (or slower if you need). It's always good to practice with a metronome to get your time together. At medium to fast tempos set the metronome to click on beats 1 & 3. Also practice with it clicking on 2 & 4.

Solo Ideas for <u>Well You Needn't</u>
Using the Minor Sub Approach

Track #17-18

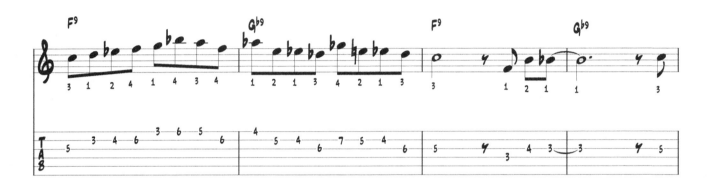

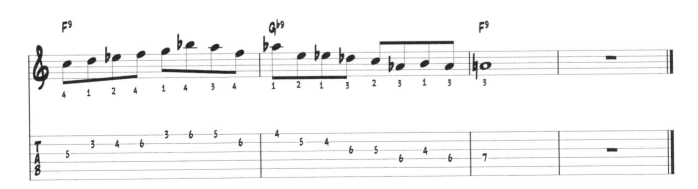

13

Tip from Dave: Try playing this exercise in octaves ala Wes Montgomery. Also learn this (and all the exercises in the book) in different keys, octaves and positions on the neck.

MINOR SUB ARPEGGIO BLUES EXERCISE

DAVE STRYKER

HERE IS AN EXERCISE ON A BLUES IN "F" USING THE MINOR SUB APPROACH, ONLY THIS TIME WITH ARPEGGIO (CHORD TONE) IDEAS.

Track #19-20

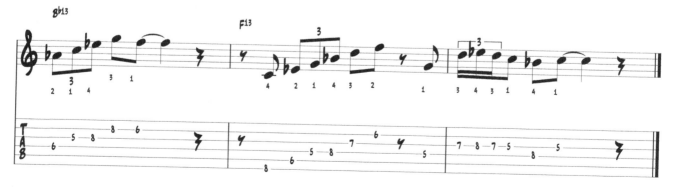

14

MINOR SUB ARPEGGIO BLUES WITH 1/2 STEP APPROACH

Dave Stryker

On this example instead of staying on F7 for four bars I've used a half-step approach on the chords. I approach each chord from a half-step above it and continue throughout. Then I matched the corresponding minor sub arpeggio to each chord.

Track #21-22

Tip from Dave: Try using this half-step chord approach on other tunes you play. It gives you a modern sound when you lead into the next chord from the same chord or a dominant chord a 1/2 step above. (Herbie Hancock uses this sometimes.)

15

Blues #1

Dave Stryker

This melody can be played chord melody style using the notes in the basic chords, without having to move the fingers of your left hand out of the chord form.

Track #23-24

Blues #1 Solo Using Minor Sub Approach

Dave Stryker

17

F Blues Scale

Dave Stryker

Track #25

BLUES IN F NO. 2

This is a one chorus blues solo that incorporates the F blues sound as well as some bebop phrases. Note the C- phrase against the F13 chord in measures 3 & 4: a II–V going to Bb. Also in measures 9 & 10 there is a good II–V phrase.

Dave Stryker

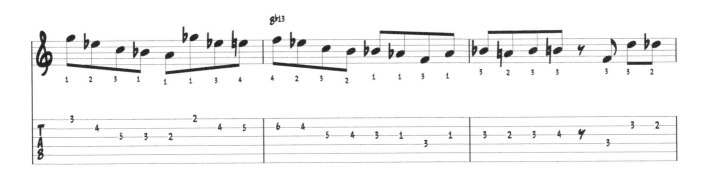

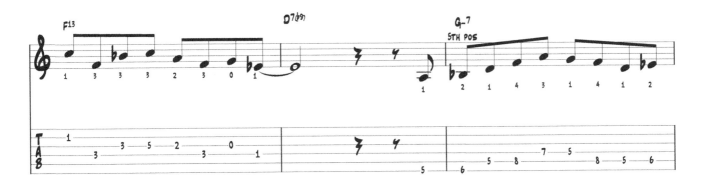

Tip from Dave: Learn the G- phrase in measures 9 + 10 in different keys and positions. Then try it on a modal type tune like "Milestones" or "So What" by Miles Davis.

Blues in F No. 3

Dave Stryker

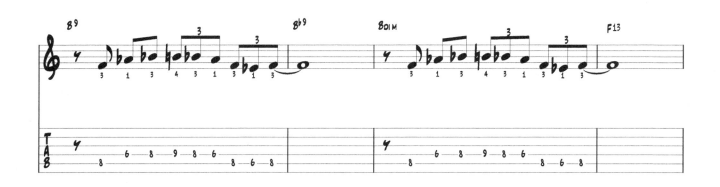
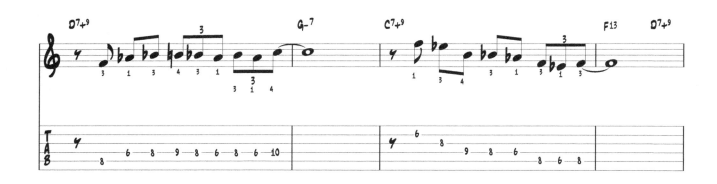
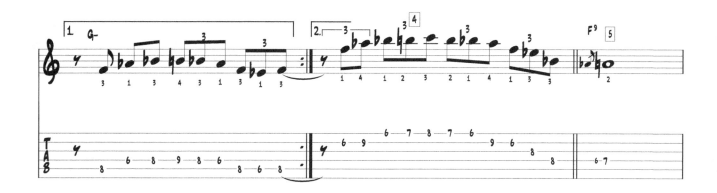

Blues in F No. 3 (Points of Interest)

1. Simplicity

2. Feeling

3. Same melody (although simple) creates tension over different chords

4. 2nd ending forceful entry into solo ala Grant Green

5. A natural nails the F7 chord

6. F#-9 phrase works over B7

7. Resolves to D (nails the Bb7)

8. Diminished run ala Jack McDuff

9. Good turnaround on A-

10. Bb triad over G-

11. Bring it home with the blues

Using the Blues Scale and Minor Arpeggios for Solo Ideas on Song for My Father

Some songs lend themselves to using the blues scale. Another idea is to use minor arpeggios from the Minor Sub Approach.

Dave Stryker

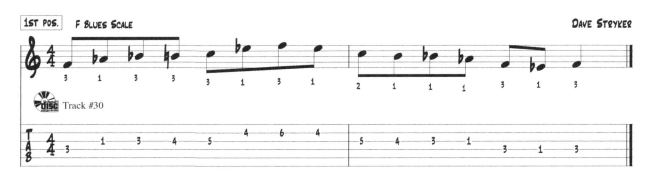

F minor arpeggio can be used on F-, Bb7, DbMa7, Dmin7b5, AbMaj7

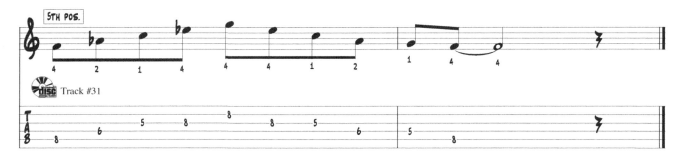

22

SOLO IDEAS FOR <u>SONG FOR MY FATHER</u>

Dave Stryker

Track #32-33

Tip from Dave: Play the second chorus of the solo (when it goes to the minor arpeggio ideas) in octaves. It helps to build your solo like Wes Montgomery would when he started his solos using single-line ideas, moved to octaves and finished with chords.

PENTATONIC SCALES

The five note pentatonic scale is often used in jazz improvisation, and creates a bluesy sound. There are also many patterns that can be derived from this scale. When combined with bebop phrases while "playing the changes", pentatonics can add another color to your improvisation.

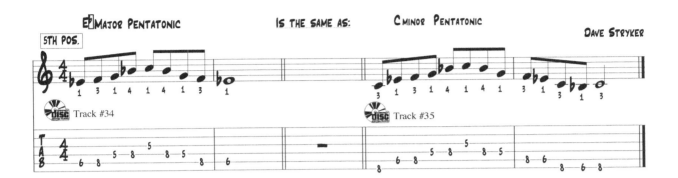

To play over C minor, go up a minor third from C and play the Eb Major Pentatonic scale
(C- play Eb Major Pentatonic)

Here is a solo over "Blue Bossa" using some pentatonic ideas and patterns.
ON: C- Use C minor pentatonic (Eb Major Pentatonic)
   F- Use F minor pentatonic (Ab Major pentatonic)
   /Dmin7b5 G7+ / C- / Use C minor pentatonic
   /Eb- Ab7/   Use Eb minor pentatonic
   Db Major   Use Db, Ab or Eb Major pentatonic (for a lydian sound)

25

Solo Ideas for Blue Bossa
Using Pentatonic Scales and Patterns

Dave Stryker

Track #36-37

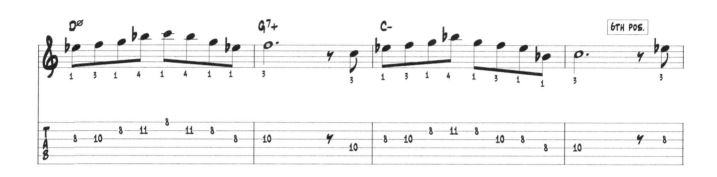

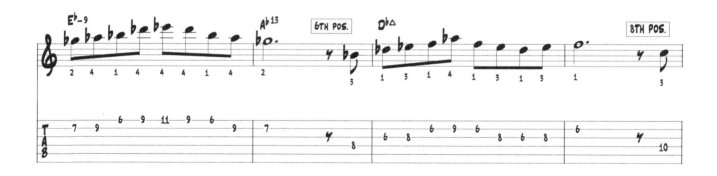

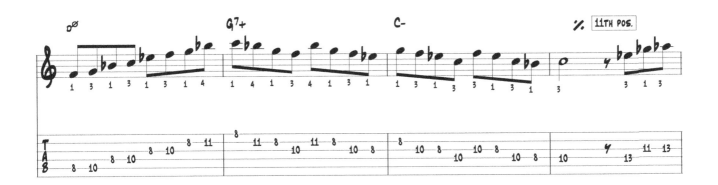

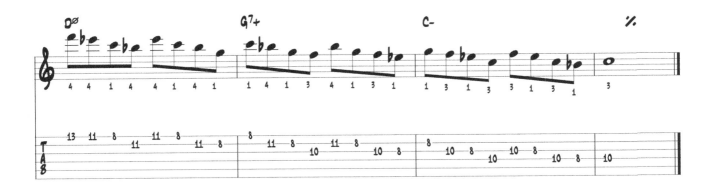

Tip from Dave: Use these pentatonic patterns on other tunes like "Song for My Father" or "So What."

27

Turnarounds & Bebop Phrases

Dave Stryker

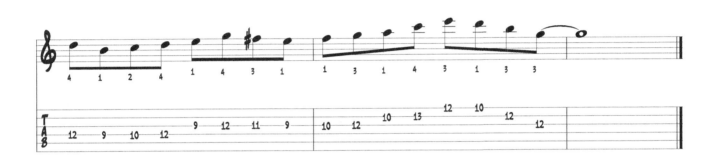

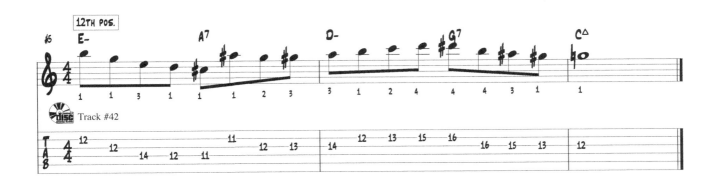

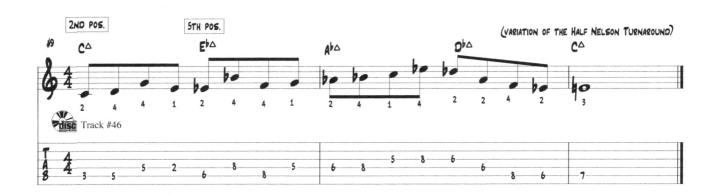

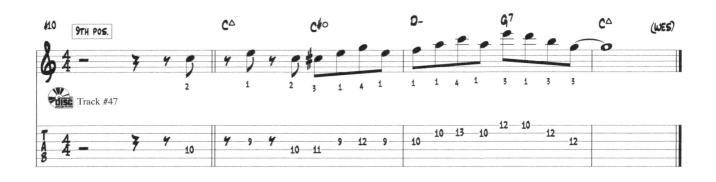

After silence, that which comes nearest to expressing the inexpressible is music.
- Aldous Huxley

Music is your own experience, your own thoughts, your wisdom. If you don't live it, it won't come out of your horn. They teach you there's a boundary line to music. But, man, there's no boundary line to art.
- Charlie Parker

If ya ain't got it in ya, ya can't blow it out.
- Louis Armstrong

Music is the silence between the notes.
- Claude Debussy

What's best in music is not to be found in the notes.
- Gustav Mahler

[Music] takes us out of the actual and whispers to us dim secrets that startle our wonder as to who we are, and for what, whence, and whereto.
- Ralph Waldo Emerson

Jazz is my adventure.
- Thelonious Monk

I am enough of an artist to draw freely upon my imagination. Imagination is more important than knowledge. Knowledge is limited. Imagination encircles the world.
- Albert Einstein

Genius is one percent inspiration and ninety-nine percent perspiration.
- Thomas Edison

Only in men's imagination does every truth find an effective and undeniable existence. Imagination, not invention, is the supreme master of art as of life.
- Joseph Conrad

Solo Ideas for <u>Afternoon in Paris</u> Using Bebop Phrases & Turnarounds

Dave Stryker

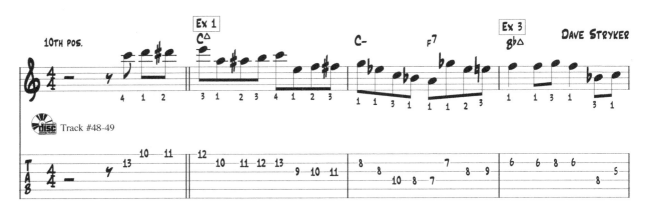

Track #48-49

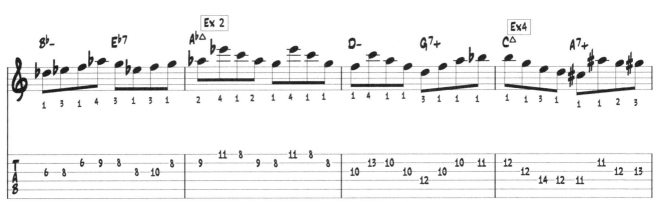

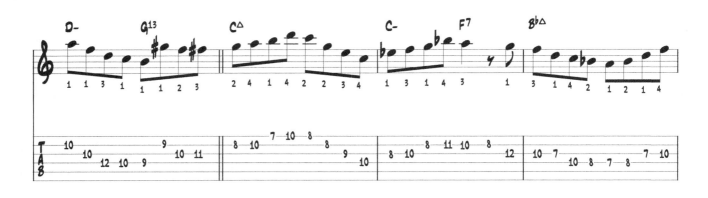

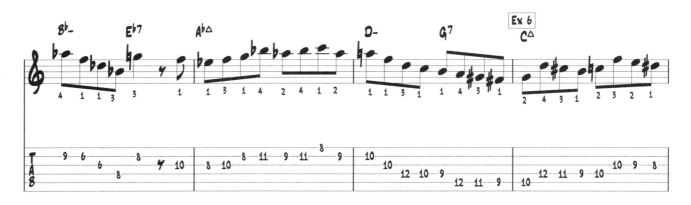

Tip from Dave: Use the Half-Nelson phrase (the last two bars of the solo) as a turnaround in other songs. Use the turnarounds and bebop phrases combined with your own ideas to build up your bebop vocabulary. Also memorize as many Charlie Parker melodies as you can.

THE MELODIC MINOR SCALE

Dave Stryker

Here is a C melodic minor scale (C minor - dorian - scale with a major 7th, also called F Lydian ♭7)

Use on: Cmin/maj7, F13+11, F7♭5, G/E♭, E♭maj7+5, B7+, B7+9. Also use on regular C minor chord to create tension.

Track #50

EX 1

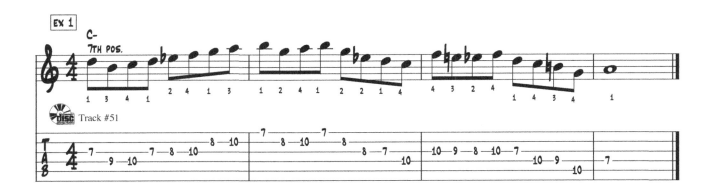

Track #51

EX 2

Track #52

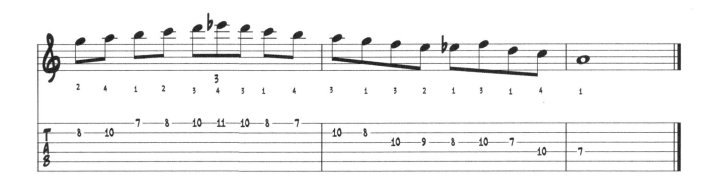

34

WHOLE-TONE SCALES & PATTERNS

Dave Stryker

A whole-tone scale is a scale built in whole steps.

Uses of the whole-tone scale:

Use on G7+ (or any aug. chord built on a note of this scale), can be used as a passing chord to C minor or C major. You can also use Ab melodic minor on G7+ .

Track #54

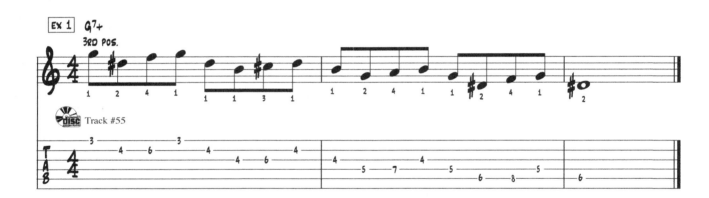

Ex 1 G7+
3rd pos.
Track #55

Ex 2 G7+
Track #56

EX 3

Track #57

Ex 4

B AUGMENTED ARPEGGIO (ALSO WORKS OVER G7+ AND A7b5)

6TH POS.

Track #58

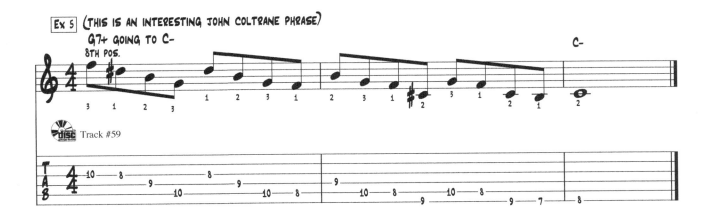

Ex 5 (THIS IS AN INTERESTING JOHN COLTRANE PHRASE)

G7+ GOING TO C-

8TH POS.

C-

Track #59

Tip from Dave: Listen to horn players like John Coltrane, Sonny Rollins and Miles Davis. Playing saxophone lines on guitar can lead to some fresh and interesting ideas.

DIMINISHED SCALES & PATTERNS

Dave Stryker

THE SCALE IS PLAYED: HALF-STEP/WHOLE-STEP/HALF-STEP/WHOLE-STEP, ETC.

1. ON C7+9, PLAY THE SCALE STARTING A HALF-STEP FROM C:

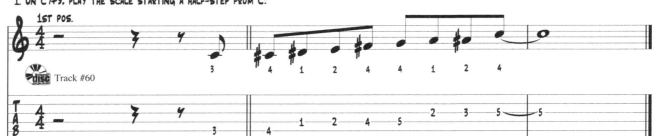

Track #60

2. ON C DIM. OR B/C PLAY THE SCALE STARTING A WHOLE-STEP FROM C:

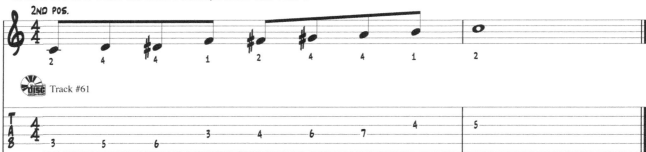

Track #61

3. HERE'S AND IDEA THAT USES A DIMINISHED ARPEGGIO AGAINST A C^o CHORD.

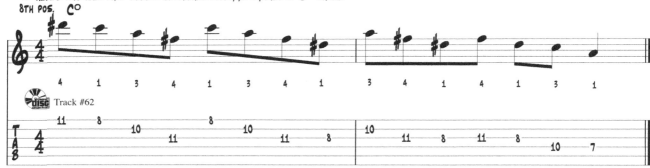

Track #62

4. C7+9 BASIC SCALE:

8TH POS.

Track #63

5. HERE'S A COLTRANE TYPE IDEA:
8TH POS.

Track #64

(Not shown in tab)

6.
3RD POS.

Track #65

7.
8TH POS.

Track #66

8.
8TH POS.

Track #67

C Minor Blues

Dave Stryker

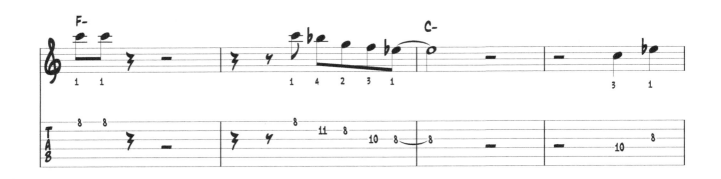
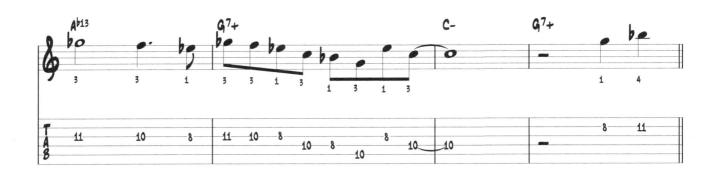

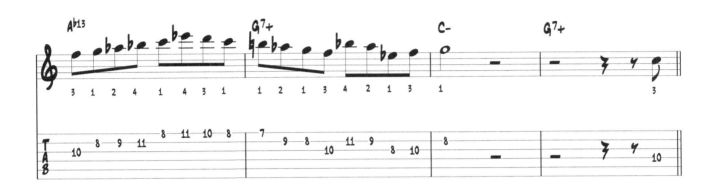

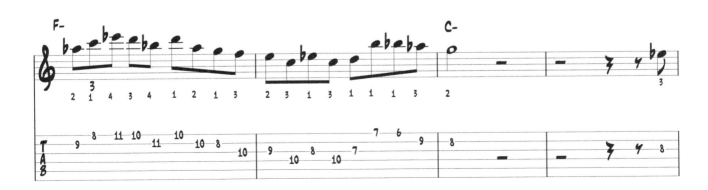

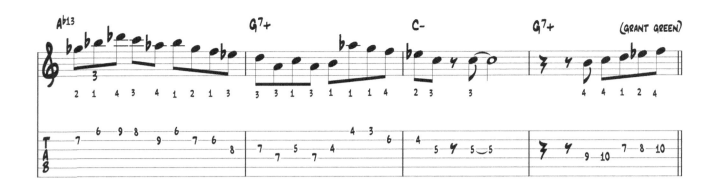

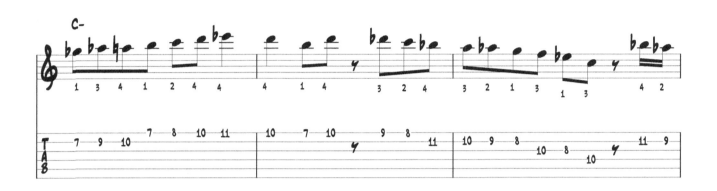

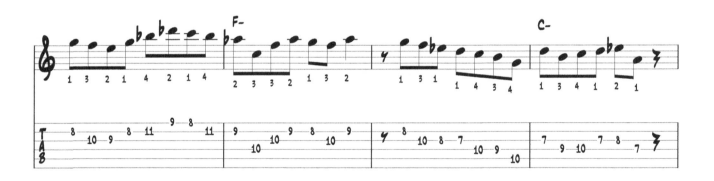

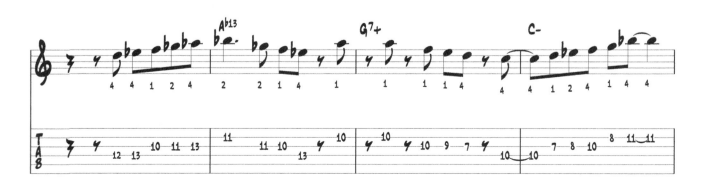

Tip from Dave: On this solo I incorporated some ideas I use when playing over a minor blues. The fourth chorus is part of a solo that Grant Green played on the song "Minor League" on the album *Solid*. Try transposing solos of players you like to get new ideas. You'll see your playing improve.

Solo Ideas for All The Things You Are

Dave Stryker

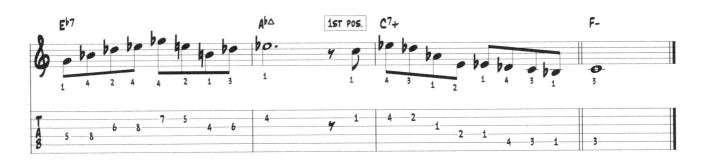

Tip from Dave: This solo over "Rhythm Changes" contains some great bebop lines. Try extracting two or four bar phrases to practice and use in your own solos. Bars 9-12 contain a classic Charlie Parker run. On the bridge I used the tri-tone/ii-v, substitute changes I've heard saxophonist George Coleman play. Therefore on the second bar of the bridge I play an Ab7 or (Eb-Ab7) instead of D7 and continue that idea throughout the bridge. Also learn this solo in F, as F and Bb are the two most common keys for "Rhythm Changes."

SOLO IDEAS FOR (I GOT) RHYTHM CHANGES

Dave Stryker

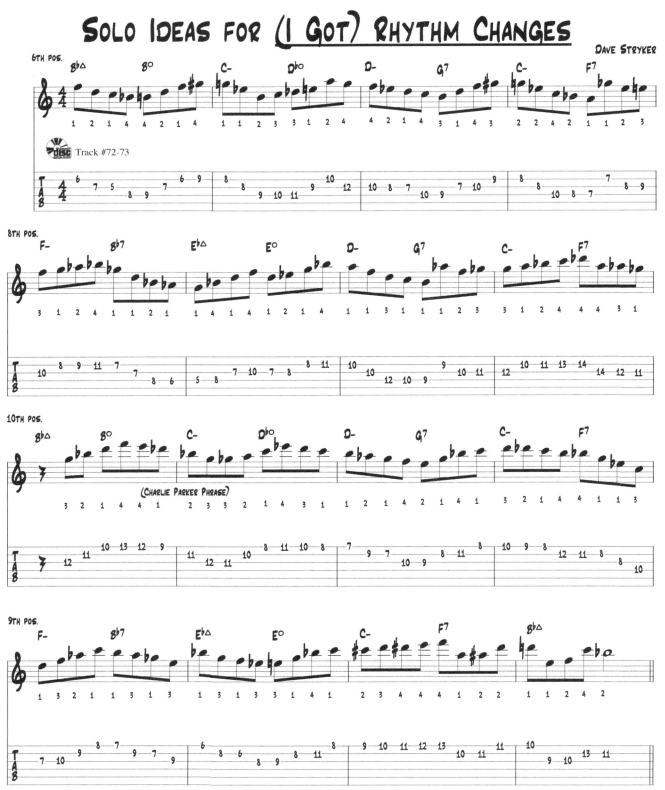

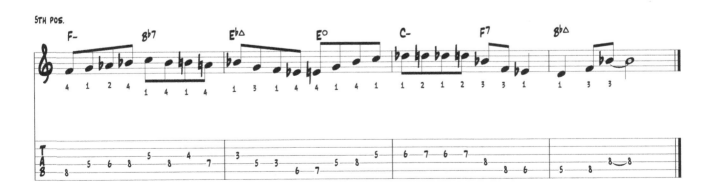

Tip from Dave: Here is another classic bebop tune. Try using ideas from different "A" sections to create your own solos. Try playing this tune fast! On fast tempos set your metronome to click on beats one and three. How about ♩=138? Good Luck!

Solo Ideas for Cherokee

Dave Stryker

Track #74-75

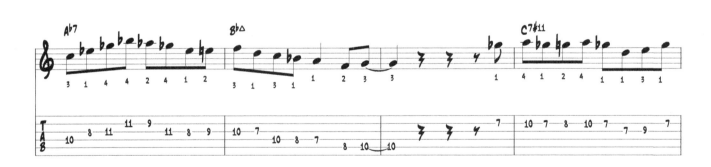

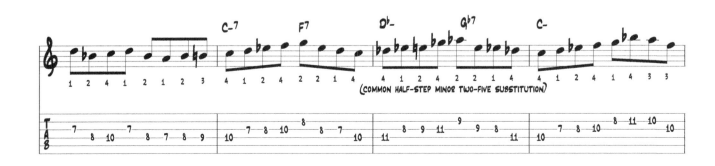

(COMMON HALF-STEP MINOR TWO-FIVE SUBSTITUTION)

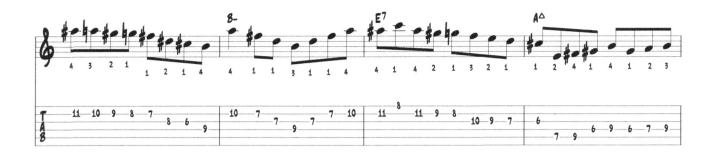

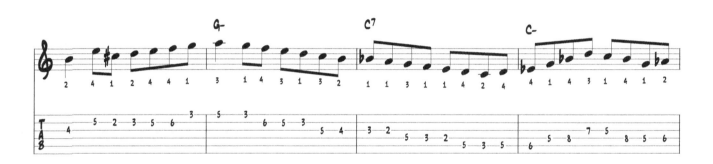

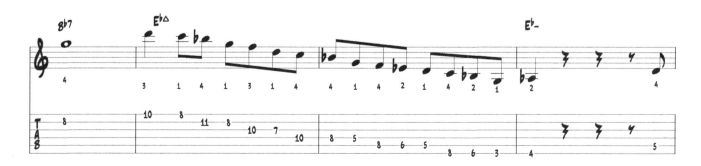

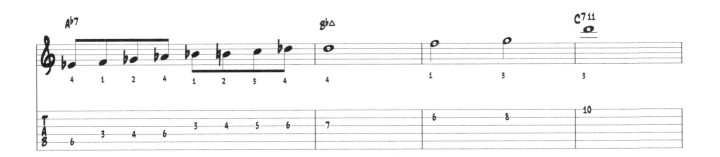

Tip from Dave: Well you've made it this far to the "Holy Grail", "Giant Steps!" At this point let me just say once again that the key to improving and moving up to the next "rung on the ladder" in your playing, lies in transcribing solos. I really feel you must do this to become a great player. As a matter of fact, the last measure of this solo happens to be the beginning of Coltrane's solo on "Giant Steps."

Have Fun!

GIANT STEPS

DAVE STRYKER

HERE ARE SOME SOLO IDEAS FOR PLAYING THROUGH A MORE DIFFICULT TUNE LIKE GIANT STEPS

PLAY THE 1ST, 2ND, 3RD AND FIFTH SCALE TONE OF EACH CHORD:

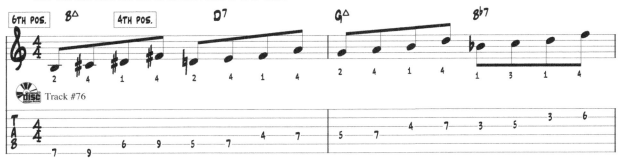

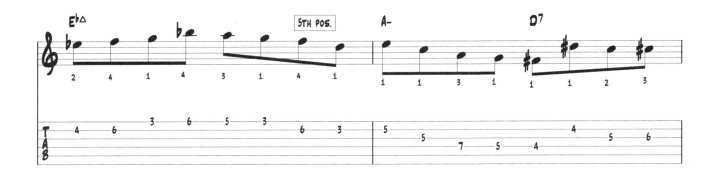

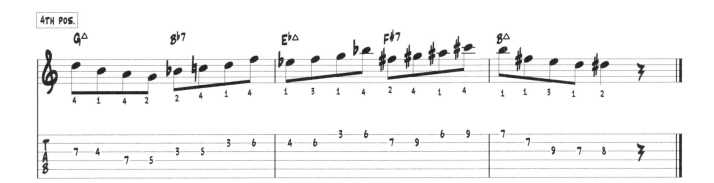

USE THE MINOR SUB APPROACH SO D7 BECOMES A-, Bb7 BECOMES F-, ETC. IF THE BASS PLAYS THESE SUBSTITUTE CHORDS THEN THE BASS LINE MOVES DOWN IN WHOLE STEPS. COLTRANE USED THIS FORM OF GIANT STEPS CHANGES ON "BUT NOT FOR ME".

Track #77-78

53

Tip from Dave: I use these exercises to get my fingers warmed up and moving every time I pick up my guitar. Play these exercises slowly with a metronome and gradually build up the tempo. Also keep playing each exercise all the way up the neck. I use alternate picking usually. Your fingers should be loose and ready to go after doing these exercises for 15 minutes.

HANON-TYPE WARM-UP EXERCISES FOR GUITAR
Dave Stryker

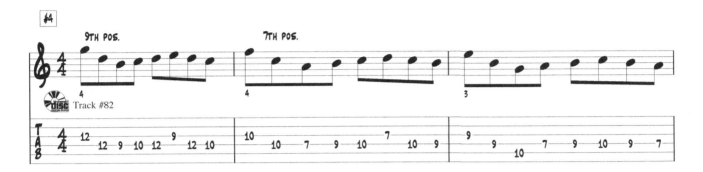

55

Dave Stryker

Whether you've heard guitarist Dave Stryker fronting his own group (with 18 CD's as a leader to date), or as a featured sideman with Stanley Turrentine, Jack McDuff, and Kevin Mahogany, you know why Gary Giddins in the Village Voice calls him *"one of the most distinctive guitarists to come along in recent years."* He was voted one of the Top Ten Guitarists in the 2001 Critics and Readers Poll and a Rising Star in the 2004 Downbeat Magazine Critics Poll. His approach combining the jazz burn to a soulful blues feeling is communicating to new fans wherever he plays.

Stryker grew up in Omaha, Nebraska and moved to New York City in 1980. After establishing himself in the local music scene, he joined organist Jack McDuff's group, travelling all over the U.S. for two years (1984-85). From 1986 to 1995, Stryker played with tenor saxophonist Stanley Turrentine, performing at all the major festivals, concert halls, and clubs throughout the world. He is featured on two Turrentine CDs and with Stanley, Stryker was able to play with jazz greats Dizzy Gillespie and Freddie Hubbard. Over ten years playing alongside the tenor legend helped Dave realize the importance of having his own sound.

Stryker recorded his first CD *First Strike* in 1988. *Guitar on Top* (1991) reached #13 on the Gavin Radio Chart and received 4 1/2 stars in Downbeat magazine. Articles on Dave have appeared in *Downbeat, Guitar Player, JazzTimes, Swing Journal,* and *Jazz Life,* and he has been awarded three Jazz grants from the National Endowment for the Arts.

In 1990 Dave began his association with SteepleChase Music. Since them he has released 15 CD's including *Strikezone, Passage, Blue Degrees, Full Moon, Stardust, Nomad* (with the Bill Warfield Big Band), *The Greeting, Blue to the Bone I , II and III, Big Room, All the Way, Changing Times* and *Shades of Miles.* Another recent project is Trio Mundo - *Carnaval* on (Khaeon) with percussionist Manolo Badrena. Stryker's most recent CD *Blue to the Bone III* was voted one of the top CD's of 2002 by NY/NJ Radio station WBGO and by *Jazzreview. Shades Beyond* featuring drummer Lenny White is his 2004 release on SteepleChase, and "Big City" is his 2005 release on Mel Bay Records.

Early on Stryker realized that as much as he loved playing standards and the jazz repertoire he had to have something of his own to give to the music. He feels that his writing combined with his playing is what shapes his musical expression. He has recorded and published over eighty of his own compositions. Eighteen of those compositions (from the first five SteepleChase CD's) are compiled in the book: *The Music of Dave Stryker* (SteepleChase Music). Some of the other artists who have recorded his music are: Stanley Turrentine, Kevin Mahogany, Victor Lewis and Steve Slagle.

Dave continues to perform with his working unit *The Stryker / Slagle Band* as well as his other projects: *The Blue to the Bone Band, The Shades Project* (w/ Lenny White), and his latest group *Trio Mundo,* featuring Manolo Badrena on percussion and vocals and Andy McKee on bass. Recent gigs for The Stryker / Slagle Band have included the Monterey Jazz Festival, The Blue Note in Las Vegas, The Jazz Bakery in LA, and a 2003 tour of Japan.

Recent sideman work has included vocalist Kevin Mahogany's group, with Dave writing and arranging music for Kevin's latest Telarc release *Pride and Joy* and *Another Time, Another Place* on Warner Bros, and tours of Europe, Japan, Brazil, Poland and Carnegie Hall. He also has worked with Blue Note saxophonist Javon Jackson and pianist Eliane Elias. He has appeared on over 40 CD's as a sideman.

As a producer, Stryker compiled the CD *The Guitar Artistry of Billy Rogers* which is the only existing record of the brilliant jazz playing of the late underground legend who was his friend, former teacher and member of the Crusaders. He has also produced *A Tribute to Grant Green* on Evidence Music and most recently produced *Trio Mundo* and the upcoming *Trio Mundo Rides Again* (ZOHO Music). Dave is also involved in teaching both privately and at Outreach Jazz Workshop in Austria, Litchfield Jazz Fest Summer Music School and the Aebersold Summer Jazz Workshop.

Dave Stryker
www.davestryker.com

Made in the USA
Columbia, SC
09 November 2020